Women of the Bible

the good, the bad, & ugly...

then and now

BY DR. SHARON CANNON

Be Blessed!
Ler. Sharon A. Cannon
Mark 11:24

Women of the Bible: the good, the bad & ugly

...then and now

By

Dr. Sharon A. Cannon

4-P Publishing

Chattanooga, TN

The Women of the Bible: the good, the bad & ugly

...then and now

First Edition: August 2014

Printed in the United States of America

ISBN 978-1-941749-10-4

4-P Publishing

Chattanooga, TN

TO

My parents who gave me life; to my children for headaches, heartaches and happiness; to my grandchildren for patience and understanding of *home alone*; my brothers and sisters for just being siblings ;to my aunts and uncles and other family members who always knew I was special; to my dearly missed grandparents who planted the seeds and nurtured me to grow; to my church families that taught me method, structure and helped me discover my purpose and presented me the opportunity to serve; to my brothers in the word who offered to help; to my spiritual sisters who gave me encouragement when I needed it most; to my reviewers who inspired me to "keep pushing"; to my illustrator "SEVEN " who made my pictures "artistic" and to all others who were good, bad and ugly to me, you truly were the source of my endurance.

Preface

A woman should not be ashamed of who or what she has done whether it be good, bad or ugly. This book was solely written as a research thesis paper for my Doctorate of Religious Education. The title at the onset was "Women of the Bible The Good, The Bad, The Ugly Yesterday and Today". When the time came to defend the thesis before the candidate committee there were no females who had read it or on the committee. Therefore the committee recommended that the degree be conferred. The next step was to get published so what you can expect in this book:

a) Title change

b) Research questionnaire & data

c) Readings about women some good, bad and ugly

d) An opportunity to enhance your Bible study/Devotion

Introduction

The role of women in churches has become so visual and profound to individuals who are on the outside looking in. As the church makes its way into the twenty-first century it brings with it a cyclical effect of what went on over 2,000 years ago. The Lord has not changed He still works in mysterious ways and his works cannot be challenged or matched. It is true from the Scriptures where the harvest is plentiful and the laborers are few and a total prophetic spin is about to take place within the church with women, their roles and responsibilities. In times past many of the leadership roles were held by men. However, there were and have always been women in the background really contributing to the success and in some cases failure of men in leadership positions. The world is about to experience a transition of women in power nationally. But these titles and positions from a biblical sense have always existed for women. Through the profiles of biblical women I want to show the good, the bad and the ugly. To know Jesus in a personal way was special then as well as now. Sharing the relationship with Jesus as it relates to family and the numerous female friends he had relationships with who could be termed as the enemy have many similar qualities from the professions to businesses and definitely serving in the church as missionaries, deaconesses and ministers. There comes a time when the Holy Spirit has to have his way with you personally as a woman and when God speaks we must listen. In order to be aware of what is going on around you, you must be prepared with your shield and armor. None of these things mentioned could prepare you for the wiles of the world and how to defend yourself without daily devotion. This thesis turned book is an opportunity for me to share my faith, beliefs and hopes. It helps me validate who I am as a woman in the word but most important "Whose I am".

Contents

CHAPTER 1

PROFILES OF BIBLICAL WOMEN

Women have always been interested in other women. They have admired the way they look, how they carry themselves and their attitudes. So it is all fitting that we as women of the word should model ourselves from the profiles of biblical women. Yes, there are the good, the bad, and the ugly in all women and I want to be the first to say that these traits can be found in me as well.

The Good

One of the first women in the Old Testament that stands out as a "good" biblical woman is **Ruth**. Ruth a Moabite must have been a very beautiful young lady and an unusually friendly lady as her name means "friendship" or "beauty".

Those good qualities of Ruth were exhibited by her devotion to her mother-in-law Naomi by not leaving her, but following her back to her country. The profound message from Ruth that stands out is her relationship with Naomi. To examine this relationship further we see the history between these two ladies because of Ruth's marriage to Naomi's son. However, the son dies and this woman named Ruth tells the mother-in-law that "your people shall be my people, and your God, my God" Ruth 1:16. Ruth was an extraordinary woman because she showed loyalty and love to her mother-in-law to which some women of today have no commitment. The mere essence of an in-law of any kind makes many women cringe and resentful of their spouses family as a whole. However, Ruth was rewarded with the introduction to Boaz and the love story saga continues.

Ruth showed more good qualities my minding her own business as she gleaned in the fields. She caught the eye of Boaz and he immediately realized that she was a relative after talking to his foreman of the fields. Boaz of course showed her special favor but the most humbling opportunity for Ruth was exhibited when "Boaz explained that he had heard of her extraordinary faithfulness to Naomi and the great sacrifices she had made to come to a foreign land". The Lord really has a way of rewarding you when you do his will and Ruth was truly rewarded in fact she received a blessing from Boaz, but she being very lady like accepted, but told him in so many words that she is not like his other maid servants. This is when a courtship begins because Ruth is invited to dine with his workers and Boaz made sure she had plenty to eat. Why of course good girls get tempted too, but how you resist is the key.

Sometimes people can get in your business such as Naomi getting into Ruth's by encouraging her to play the game of getting Boaz to marry her. The incident of Ruth following Naomi's instructions and waking up at the feet of Boaz was not immoral, nothing happened but Boaz being the man he was did send her home.

The story of Ruth and her good qualities as a God-fearing woman produced offspring that Naomi got credit for because her daughter-in-law truly showed loyalty and love.

Hannah's name means "grace". In the Old Testament we heard of many women who longed to have children. The mere essence of becoming a mother overtook Hannah as it did many others. They knew that their marriages were in jeopardy because their husbands strayed and fathered children with other women. But a praying woman that Hannah was paid off in exceedingly and wonderful ways with the son she so desired. This precious child was prayed for and being careful for what she prayed for she had included a promise that she would give him back. This prayer that Hannah prayed was called a dedicatory prayer, when she offered her son to God, was actually a prophetic prayer to Israel's Messiah. Although when we look at Hannah's vow through the prayer, we find that it was in two parts. One was the promise to give the child to the Lord where subsequent events indicated that by this pledge she intended to devote him to full time service in the tabernacle.

Her visit to the tabernacle to leave her son had to be hard but the transition of knowing that she had trained Samuel up right and keeping the vow she made to the Lord was the most important. No person in Israel surpassed Hannah in intelligence, beauty and fervor of devotion to God. Hannah's prayer was not an act of bargaining, but an act of surrender. In giving up control of her most precious son to God (to whom he already belonged), Hannah found inner peace.

Hannah like so many women in the Bible always traveled each year to the tabernacle in Shiloh to worship and do a sacrifice. A description of Hannah states not only was she the quintessential godly mother and wife, but in a spiritually cold generation she exemplified patience, prayerfulness, faith, meekness, submission, spiritual devotion, and motherly love. One would have to show all those attributes to put up with Peninah the other wife of Elkanah. The teasing and cruel treatment that others gave women in those days was awful. But when you have the Lord on your side as Hannah did there was no need to worry because the Lord did supply all her needs.

Many stories have been told of some famous person who rose from rags to riches; this seems almost the story of **Esther**. Why of course the story goes on to tell how she rose to be one of the most powerful women in the Bible because of her faith. Esther's sweet spirit and personality matched her physical attractiveness. So there was no question that when there was an opportunity for the king to pick a queen that Esther was available for the position. What is fascinating is how this young woman respected her uncle Mordecai and continually accepted his guidance. When the opportunity came for her to step out in faith Esther determined to do as Mordecai asked, and she approached her husband. Her statement "If I perish, I perish", is not a fatalistic abandonment but a conscious trusting of herself into God's hands. It is amazing how customs can keep love from developing. The law forbade a Jew marrying a gentile, but it is evident that Mordecai and Esther saw this union as being a blessing to their people, which it proved to be so but it still did not disannul the Word of God. When the king saw her, she obtained grace and favor in his sight and loving her above all the women he set the royal crown upon her head and made her his queen. So when Esther identified herself as a Jew begging the king for her own life and for that of her people, throughout this account we see Esther winning the favor of those in authority.   A quiet, submissive spirit; obedient actions; and wise choices made her stand out from their society, even as it would make each of us stand out today.

There are more good women in the Bible who are identified in the New Testament. A remarkable lady, whose name is **Eunice** means "happily victorious", which so aptly describes her person. Eunice was known for her son Timothy and he was a close companion of Paul the missionary. Eunice, as many mothers, taught her son Scripture from childhood. She saw him saved while he was young. To have godly parents is a blessing and Eunice as a mother exhibited a real commitment to scripture and prayer not only for herself but to her child. All of this is needed because you have to accept what your children do. But it is far more common for parents to experience heartache along the way as boys and girls disappoint us. Yes, our children know how to push our buttons but when parents are well grounded and rooted in the word they are victorious. The influence of godly Eunice should be an inspiration for any woman to be a more godly mother. Mothers need to be more like Eunice and be careful to walk before their children in godliness with genuine faith. Eunice had all the makings of a good woman in biblical times and her characteristics should be adapted by women in the world today.

Earlier I stated that some of the good women were Ruth, Hannah, Esther and Eunice. There were others who were good such as **Rachel**. Rachel was the sister of Leah the "hussy" that tricked her way into the arms of Jacob so she thought. A little background of the story tells how Jacob was at a well in Haran and saw Rachel coming to water her animals. He asked some of the men who she was and they told him her name is "Rachel" and she is the daughter of Laban. Jacob knew that was a family name on his mothers side, so that made Rachel his cousin. He went up to her giving her the news and this is what you call "Love" at first sight. Rachel took Jacob back to meet Laban and he told Laban that he had fallen in love with his daughter and asked to marry her and by his asking he knew he would have to work seven years for her. The Scriptures say: "And Laban said, it is better that I give her to thee, than that I should give her to another man; abide with me." (Gen. 29:19)

Well the time went by fast and before Jacob knew it he was asking Laban to give Rachel to him for marriage. This is when the scheme is conspired with Leah. There is going to be some sister swapping on the wedding night.

The morning after the marriage when Jacob discovers what has happened everything goes into disarray. Jacob confronts Laban about Rachel and Laban makes excuses about how it is not proper to give the younger before the elder. Jacob didn't want to hear that stuff. He wanted to know what he had to do to get Rachel and of course Laban said work another seven years. All of this time Rachel has been sitting back watching what was going on, now a *real sister* would have been up in the middle and causing true chaos, saying: "This is the man I love and you think you can get away with this you must be crazy!" Rachel, however, was a true lady, she held her peace, this puts her in the "good" category. Although Rachel was a beautiful young lady, kind and gracious, her personality was more or less a mixed personality. In the story of her life, we read of her sins of falsehood to her father; her envy and jealousy of her sister and of her stealing idols for worship, none of which is becoming to a child of God.

Today's woman relative to being "good" might be that woman working in the Church when the doors open and when they close serving on committees and being everything to everybody. But she too has a story to tell how she didn't have food and one day a box of food appeared at the door to feed her family and now she volunteers to distribute food monthly to others. We see her "good works" but we don't know her spirit. She could be the spiritual leader in the church of "doing the right things" and she is in the community working to bring others into the church. That *good* woman could be an everyday woman without a title or position but has a personal relationship with Christ that only she and God know. Rachel is a clear example of why she is called "good." We really should not categorize women of today as being *good,* because the Scriptures say: "For all have sinned and come short of the glory of God." (Romans 3:23).

The Bad

Bad girls, bad girls what are you going to do next? The Bible is full of bad girls and then there are some really bad girls. The first bad girl is **Eve**. It is true that God took this woman, this lovely, beautiful creature, made especially for Adam and gave her to him.[18]

So what could be so wrong with the first marriage? All the rules were given of what and what not to touch or eat. Eve listened to the serpent and yielded to the temptation of eating the forbidden fruit from the tree of knowledge. Howbeit, God brought a curse upon her of painful childbearing and submissiveness to her husband and consequently all women ever since have been brought under this curse.

Is it really fair to say that sweet innocent Eve was a bad girl because of what she did? Eve was able to distinguish right from wrong for she told the serpent, "God has said, 'you shall not eat in, nor shall you touch it, lest you die'" (Gen. 3:3). We have to learn that we cannot get into a debate with Satan. We can't stop the adversary from whispering in our ears, but we can refuse to listen, and we can definitely refuse to respond. No arguing, and debating! Like Eve we'll come out the loser. Let's stand and resist. "Just Say No." If he doesn't fall, we can take off running for the safety of the Lord's arms. This was the first bad girl in the Bible because of her disobedience her punishments not only included childbearing but she was banished from the garden.

Potiphar's wife didn't have a name mentioned in the Scriptures. She was simply identified as Potiphar's wife who had a desire to share passion with innocent Joseph. Many women have affairs and along with it come planning, secrets and lying. Potiphar's wife played a small but notorious role in Joseph's life. She tried to seduce him and when he refused her advances, she accused him of trying to rape her, and Joseph was imprisoned. Isn't that just like some women, when one doesn't get her way she cries rape. Potiphar's wife had a way of intimidating men, because of who her husband was. I'm sure the servants felt intimidated by her and may have been caught up in her antics in the past. It is very unfortunate for Joseph that he even got that close to such a vile woman. It is obvious that Potiphar's wife was a bad girl because she was so flirtatious. The woman was not subduing. As the wife of a powerful man, she was clearly accustomed to getting exactly what she wanted. And what she wanted was Joseph, hubby's handsome slave. As a foreigner, Joseph was forbidden fruit, and Potiphar's wife knew that. It was undoubtedly part of the attraction. They were complete opposites. She was older, he was younger. She was married; he was single. She was Egyptian; he was Hebrew. She had no morals; he had high morals. She worshiped the flesh; he worshiped in spirit. Potiphar's wife was not only a bad girl but she was a nasty girl. To tell lies and make up stories to cover her tracks are things a bad girl will do and it makes her down right nasty. Potiphar's wife was a true adulteress.

Sweet, sweet **Delilah** or should I say bitter sweet. Delilah is a name that means "small", "dainty". Yes, she may have been described with those adjectives but she performed in other descriptive words such as "scheming" and "distrustful." The story of Delilah that showcases her role as a bad girl can be summed up by Delilah hounding Samson for the secret of his strength. Delilah reminds us that fleshly weakness can topple even the most powerful person. The relationship between Samson and Delilah is so charismatic and reminds me of a secular song "When a Man Loves a Woman". It seems in this song that the man cannot see anything that this woman has done that seems wrong. Like in the song, in her attempts to trick Samson, she was outwitted three times. Now anyone with some common sense could see that something just wasn't right with her doing these things. In the past we have heard people say, "The devil made me do it." This snippet of the story reveals an important fact: Betraying Samson wasn't Delilah's idea. Yes, she bought into it literally. but conventional wisdom says, "Follow the money." In this case, the money led directly back to the Philistine heads of State.

They were the ones who planted the seeds of betrayal in her heart; the games people play helped Delilah with the title as a bad girl. Samson knew Delilah well and he played games three times. After the third time, Delilah continued to be persistent with her antics. From the story it's clear that she did not profess love for him but used his love for her like a cruel cattle prod. Then she said to him, "How can you say, 'I love you' when you won't confide in me?"(Judges 16:15). Well, well, well silly foolish Samson gave in. His physical strength was still in tact, but his emotional strength had shriveled up and blown away, thanks to Delilah's endless nagging. Delilah, a bad woman in every sense was a special type of the world and the world is definitely an enemy to the child of God. Delilah proved herself an enemy to the divine purpose in the life of Samson.

Jezebel a name that does not have a meaning has become synonymous with treachery and evil and is often used to label shamelessly deceitful woman. The name Jezebel is often used as a term and this woman earned her reputation. The modern day women would call her husband "hen pecked" because Jezebel ruled and ran her household. It was not easy to be a woman of the royal family in the age of kings, yet strong women like Jezebel succeeded by the force of their personalities to gain a power which enabled them to treat men as men treated women, as objects to be used for the ruler's end without consideration and without concern.

Jezebel has been named as the baddest girl in the bunch; the one whom scholars call "the wickedest woman in all the world." So it's interesting to see Jezebel paired up with Ahab who was equally evil. When it came to religion Jezebel the Phoenician princess was born rich and in charge. Her marriage to Ahab was strictly a political alliance between two nations.

She grew up as a worshipper of Baal and was determined to drive Jehovah God out of Israel and to usher in Baal and Ashram, a fertility God and Goddess of love- Eros, not agape, unfortunately. Jezebel was a determined opponent of God, set on wiping out His prophets and purging Israel of worshipers of the Lord. Jezebel looked for ways of promoting her religious beliefs so she just wiped off some of the Lords prophets. In 1 Kings 18:4, Jezebel initiated a campaign to exterminate God's prophets and threatened Elijah's life. Jezebel did her threatening to Elijah and yes he did run for his life. In the end when God restored Elijah's courage, and he was the one who announced "concerning Jezebel the Lord also spoke, saying, 'The dogs shall eat Jezebel by the wall of Jezreel'" (I Kings 21:23). Well as fate would have it Jezebel relied on her sexuality to the end. When Jehu came into Jezreel, Jezebel heard of it so she tried to use flattery on him to save her life. She painted her face, adorned her head and looked out the window of her house. Jehu accepted none of her flattery and ordered the two or three eunuchs with her at the window to throw her down. They threw her down and some of her blood was sprinkled on the wall and on the horses.

The horses trampled her under their feet. The curse placed upon her was fulfilled when the dogs, the stray dogs of the town ate her body all except her skull, her feet and the palms of her hands. Her head that through wickedness, the palms of her hands and her feet that worked wickedness were too evil for even the dogs to eat. Now that is what you call a bad girl to the bone.

In the research I gave examples of bad girls such as Eve, Potiphar's wife, Delilah and Jezebel. But there were some *really bad* girls like Bathsheba, Jael, Rebeka and Gomer. When you categorize a woman as being *bad* it's usually because it is something she has done that put her in the category. **Bathsheba,** Miss bathing beauty Bathsheba. who hangs out on roof tops exposing her birthday suit to tempt people is our next bad girl. David had just been made king and one day he looks out over his balcony and sees Bathsheba bare to the bone bathing. He inquired from his servants as to who is that fine specimen of a woman? They tell him that her name is Bathsheba and she is the wife of Uriah, one of his soldiers. Now this is when the story gets sticky. David had lots and lots of wives but he saw something else he wanted, the wife of Uriah. So David had his special time with Bathsheba with a willing consent on her part. When she had taken care of business with David she went back home.

When she didn't have her monthly menstruation she sent word to David that she was pregnant, how could this be her husband had not been home in a while. David sent a message out to the war zone telling them to send Uriah home. King David gave direct orders to Uriah to spend any time with his wife. When Uriah came home he was so concerned about his men to spend time with his wife as King David had requested of him to do and so he returned to the war zone. This is when King David puts a "hit" out on Uriah by putting him on the front lines and Uriah was killed. The Scriptures say: "And when the wife of Uriah heard that her husband was dead, she mourned for her husband. And when the mourning was past, David sent and fetched her to his house and she became his wife, and bare him a son. But the thing that David had done displeased God" (II Samuel 26-7). So much comes from this story, about adultery, cheating and scheming. This story of Bathsheba is a soap opera gone bad. She paid of course in the end when her baby died. God doesn't like for you to mess with his men. There will be no teasing and playing taking place with God's men. Why didn't she just say "no" when David approached her? Maybe it was because he was the King. As a Christian woman the men in positions cause you to be tempted. Let me rephrase this as a woman, men in leadership, be it business or church are forbidden fruit.

18

They know how to make a *good* girl go *bad.* There are many men that intimidate women and then there are those that entice. There are those that are just doing their jobs and get "caught up" in the moment. Regardless, women have the right to just say *No!* Women need not be a part of this ordeal and stay as far away as possible and in some cases leave the church if it is happening. There have been wives of ministers who have had to look out in the congregation and wonder who her spouse may have consoled or comforted for the wrong reasons. Women don't be a Bathsheba.

We have seen movies on Lifetime Television depicting the mood swings of women and why they plan to kill their spouses, lovers, co-workers and enemies. In the Bible there is a story about **Jael**. You can't really tell the story about Jael unless you go back to the story of Deborah and Barak. The background starts with the war of General Sisera at Mount Tabor and Barak and Deborah discussing what the Lord had told Barek to do at the Kishon river. But Barak wasn't sure on winning the war so he asked Deborah to go with him. Deborah was of course angry that Barak didn't trust the Lord and the Scriptures say: "And she said, I will surely go with thee: not withstanding the journey that thou takest shall not be for thine honor;

19

for the Lord shall sell Sisera into the hand of a woman. And Deborah arose, and went with Barak to Kedesh" (Judges 4:9)

So the battle went on and all the soldiers were killed, but Sisera managed to get away. There were tents in the distance that Sisera could see. Now Heber the Kenite had left the other Kenites, and pitched his tent by the great tree in Zaanannim near Kedesh. (Judges 4:11). The Kenites were a dark-skinned, Seminomadic desert tribe of farmers and metal workers who sided with the Canaanites. However, Jael's husband, Heber, whose name means "ally", had physically separated himself from his clansmen .

So Sisera walks up on the tent of Jael and orders her to hide him and bring him some milk because he was still thirsty. He told her to tell no one where he was in case someone came looking for him. Jael was no dummy, her husband Heber had always kept her informed of what was going on war-wise about the power of the Israelites and how they trusted God and she believed that the enemy of that God was a enemy of hers too. So Sisera gets under the blanket and goes to sleep. Jael is standing there wondering what to do and she very quietly took a spike and drove it through his head, killing him. Wop! Upside the head, the wicked Sisera is dead.

So as a woman who gets credit for killing Sisera Deborah or Jael? Jael's motive for killing Sisera will tell us if she was a bad girl gone mad or a good girl who was momentarily bad for a good reason. In the news for the last few weeks we hear about Christian women who have murdered their husbands and children. We don't know what was going on in the church for individuals to decide to commit murder. There are women like Jael who seize the moment to do wrong only because they have to protect themselves. We as women again are labeled and stereotyped as being bad but a lot of times it's for a reason and only for a season.

Rebekah, was a *bad* girl and her story raises uncomfortable issues about marriage and motherhood. Her actions were designed to assist God's plan for her family; but her methods leave much to be desired. She was Isaacs's wife, and mother to Esau and Jacob .

The story of Rebekah has history of family members running things and getting into your business. Abraham and Sarah who waited for the son Isaac so long decided that he needed a wife. They were determined that he was not going to marry a Caanite woman.

So they sent out a search party to find Isaac a wife who ends up being Rebekah. She is all mixed up genealogy but she simply was the sister to Laban, (the daddy of Leah), you know from the Jacob and Leah story. Rebekah is characterized as a beautiful virgin who gladly does her share of work. Therefore she will make a suitable wife for Isaac the wife search servant party members thought. Still, the servant is not sure she is "the one". He seeks further guidance . Well the story goes on to say how the search party clarifies to Laban and Bethuel (the father of Rebekah) that God has done the matchmaking not them. However, the final decision is up to them, both Laban and Bethuel say," If God said it so it is, take her."

Well, Isaac and Rebekah were married and did not have any children of their own for a long time and then came twin boys and they named them Esau and Jacob. Esau was the hunter and Jacob was the stay at home with his mother son learning domestic duties. In biblical times the oldest son automatically inherited the birth right and this would be Esau. One day when Jacob was cooking Esau came in hungry and Jacob tricked him into selling him his birthright over a bowl of food.

As one would have it Isaac, the father, was going blind with his eyesight and he thought it was time to talk to Esau about his birthright. Isaac told Esau that he may not live much longer, so he wanted to go ahead and give him the blessing. He told Esau to go hunt and cook the meal so we can do the blessing. Rebekah overheard the conversation and she wanted Jacob to get the blessing, because she loved him more and he always stayed home with her. Rebekah came up with a plan and told Jacob about it, she knew Esau had sold his birthright years earlier to Jacob over the bowl of food. Her plan was to put sheep skins on Jacob, fix a meal and have Jacob pretend to be Esau. Isaac was half blind so how would he know? They fooled Isaac and Jacob got the blessing. But when Esau returned from his hunting trip and cooked the meal and went in to get the blessing Isaac told him that he had already given it to him. That is when they both realized that Jacob had tricked them. This angered Esau tremendously. Rebekah devises another plan, but this time to protect her precious Jacob from murder. The Scriptures say: "Now therefore my son, obey my voice; flee at once to my brother Laban in Haran, and stay with him a while, until your brother's fury turns away-until your brother's anger against you turn away, and he forgets what you have done to him; then I will send, and bring you back from there. Why should I lose both of you in one day?" (Genesis 27: 43-45).

Wow! Isn't that just like a mother? We do what we have to do to protect our children, even when they have done wrong. A mother will put the house up for bail money to get them out of jail and then they leave town or violate probation and the mother is "stuck like chuck." The motherhood of making differences bothers me in this story and yet I see it everyday with my family and others. There is always that child that seems "favored" it may be for both good and bad reasons. When there are multiple children in a family you will at one time or another devote more attention to one over the others depending on the situation. As far as Rebekah being a wife there were secrets and women do keep secrets even in a committed relationship. I have often heard don't ever let the left hand know what the right hand is doing. You know that Isaac and Esau gave her "grief" after Jacob left, I am quite sure that there was no "peace" for a long time. When a situation arises in our homes and decisions have been made relative to a family member and everyone is not on one accord we term it as "Catching H". People will not let you get over it especially if they feel you made a mistake or did not take their advice. They won't let you live it down. Rebekah was a *really bad* girl with choices that she made because they affected the entire family.

A *bad* girl that I couldn't write about extensively because she got complicated was **Gomer**. Gomer is a woman who cannot be faithful, but we never knew why. We never see her interacting with her husband, her lovers, or her children. We have no clue about her thoughts or feelings. She raises more questions for us: Was she looking for love or addicted to sex? Did she commit adultery as a rebellious act against patriarchal limits on women? How did she feel about herself? After Hosea's abuse, why did she return to him? There were too many questions to be answered about Gomer, but I know women who can relate. We have sexual assault, domestic violence and homelessness happening each and everyday. One of the reasons I couldn't write about Gomer is I didn't understand her because research states that the book of Hosea was written mainly for men, it's his testimony in directing or talking to men. Regardless, Gomer was a woman who kept silent she wasn't loud and vocal like Potiphar's wife or Jezebel. So it is safe to say that there are some women who can identify to Gomer but they just won't open up and tell it.

The Gospels are known for telling the different versions of a story in the Bible. The story of **Herodias** is told in three of the four gospels and they all have a sad ending. Herodias, "Miss Thang" yes thought she was all that and a bag of chips, she was as "flaky" as she wanted to be.

She was the daughter of Aristobulus, who was the son of Herod the Great. She abandoned her first husband, Herod Philip, for his brother, Herod Antipas. John the Baptist strongly condemned Herod for this illicit relationship, earning Herodias's hatred.

The story of Herodias is part of the John the Baptist story. John the Baptist is first introduced in Mark 1:4. John appears in the wilderness preaching and baptizing people from miles around. John's message is one of repentance and preparation for a new thing God is doing. He stands in the tradition of prophets of the Hebrew Scriptures and prepares the way for the ministry of Jesus. In Mark 1:14, we learn that John has been arrested, but we are not told why. We find out more in Mark 6.

Herod has arrested John in order to keep his wife, Herodias, from having John assassinated. John functions as a prophet and criticizes Herod and Herodias for marrying each other. John speaks out against this based on Israelite law and custom. Every time John would speak out about the dysfunction of this family it literally "ticked" Herodias off more and more. Having John in jail was not enough for her, she knew she didn't have the power to sentence him to death, so she felt a little helpless.

Herodias's bed-hopping routine started when Herod Antipas came to Rome on political, business. She decided he was more powerful of the two brothers, and so her plot to move up the political ladder was hatched. She is thinking, "I'm going to get that John so help me I am." An opportunity will soon present itself. The occasion is Herod's birthday party. He has invited all the really important folks from Galilee to the grand event.

We need to understand that there were no women at this party. It was more of a male only party and the only women in attendance, would be individuals secured to perform or do her *thing* on the dance floor. Queen Herodias, however, scores a minus ten for sending her young daughter alone into this stag party, knowing full well what it would do the girl's reputation. All Herodias cared about was making a scene and getting what she wanted, even if it did bring shame on her offspring. Add *terrible mother* to Herodias's growing list of beastly attributes.

Wow! This little girl was doing and shaking her "thang" and all the men were oohing and awing over her. The king was just thrilled that she could "shake it" and she pleased him so much.

The Scriptures say: "And when the daughter of the said Herodias came in, and danced, and pleased Herod and them that sat with him, the king said unto the damsel , ask of me whatsoever thou wilt, and I will give it thee. And he sware unto her whatsoever thou shalt ask of me, I will give it thee, unto the half of my kingdom." (Mark 6:22-23). What did he say that for? This girl nearly lost her mind, running to Herodias, "Mommy, mommy, what should I ask for?" Well, Herodias had been waiting for this day when she would have some "power."The scheming Herodias had no doubt counseled her, "After you dance for your step daddy, if he offers to give you something, track me down pronto....Prompted by her mother..." wrote Matthew. Poor Salome, could she possibly have guessed the ghastly gift her mother would ask for? "The head of John the Baptist" she answered.

Salome rushed back into the party and told the king that she wanted the head of John the Baptist. This struck a chord with the king because he didn't want to kill John, but here he was with all the guests looking at him and he didn't want to reject her request in front of everyone. He sent an executioner to the jail to behead him. The executioner brought the head on a platter, gave it to Salome and she in turn handed it to her mother, Herodias.

When the disciples heard what had happened they came and got the body and buried it in a tomb. When Jesus heard about it from the disciples he told them to separate themselves, he wanted to be by himself, but people kept following him. They wanted to be healed and taught, so Jesus had compassion and never let anyone know about the sadness he was feeling over the death of John.

Culprit, vixen, crazy, foolish are all adjectives that describe women like Herodias. They want their cake and want to eat it too. The Lord has a way of punishing women who hold grudges and desire power. I pray that the wrath of God never comes down on a woman who is against one of God's "people."

The Ugly

It has been noted that ugly is as ugly does. So when **Leah** decided to become an accomplice to her father Laban's plan this made her double ugly, ugly acting and just plain ugly. Leah, the ugly older sister Rachel and the first wife of Jacob whose name means wearied, dull, stupid, pining and yearning was tender eyed and not as beautiful nor as attractive as her sister.

When you have more than one daughter you tend to

compare the two even if they are twins and others compare them as well to state who is pretty and who is not as pretty. So we can see how Laban was concerned that his elder daughter might not be as accepting to anyone and the elder daughter in those days should marry before the others. Yes, Laban had a plan, he told Leah to keep quiet on her sister's wedding night because she was so homely no other man would want her. Leah had to be an accomplice of Laban's on the wedding night. As a man Jacob acted what we term as a "fool" when he found out what happened. Jacob did not discover her true identity until after the marriage had been consummated and so had no recourse but to accept her as his first wife. Anyone who has been married twice and have children knows what its like to have your children favored over others and vice-versa. Leah kept looking for love, approval and acceptance from Jacob and she was continually disappointed until she reoriented her life toward God. Her faithfulness won the sincere respect of Jacob and when she died he buried her in the family cemetery in Machpelah (Gen 49:31); and he asked to be buried with her. There was no personal attractiveness with Leah but her relationship with God did develop. God did love Leah, he gave her seven children and in the process God taught her to seek comfort in him.

Miriam is best known as the big sister of Moses. Her heroic antic to watch the lifeboat her mother had built to save her baby brother from the wrath of Pharoah who was killing all boy babies as they were born made her special. Miriam was 12 years old when this occurred. When Miriam saw Pharoah's daughter going to the river to bathe she saw her discover the basket. She immediately recognized the baby as a Hebrew boy baby and Miriam quickly struck up a conversation with this curious daughter of Pharoah and offered to fetch a Hebrew woman to nurse the baby. Thanks to his sisters efforts. Moses was returned to his mothers arms. So how can a sweet lovely girl such as Miriam be classified as ugly with the biblical women you may ask? She grew up to be a gracious woman of various natural gifts. She was a prophetess, the first woman who was ever endowed with the gift of prophecy. She was a great help to her brother Moses in the service of the Lord. Miriam as we have noted was an obedient daughter, a protective big sister, a prophetess and worship leader. She was not above human frailty, however, Miriam's pride got in her way. She felt jealous that Moses as a more exalted prophet than she was and led her brother Aaron into the same negative thinking. It is obvious that Miriam had "issues", she was the instigator with the golden calf and then she criticized Moses for his marriage to an "Ethiopian"

(Cushite) woman. And Miriam and Aaron spoke against Moses because of the Ethiopian women whom he married. (Numbers 12:1). Having the spiritual leader's role was not enough for Miriam. She yearned to be viewed by all as someone who was on par with Moses, not a subordinate to him.[41] Sometimes women can get too big for their britches and the "ugly" comes out. Miriam started acting ugly and you don't mess with God's people. Miriam reminds us that jealousy and pride stand in the way of our fellowship with God. These traits also keep God from using us to minister to others. So what did God do to keep Miriam in order? Anger can be defined as a strong feeling of belligerence aroused by a real or supposed inequality. God's anger was kindled against Miriam and Aaron when they talked against Moses because of his Ethiopian wife. Miriam became leprous.

After God chastised Miriam we never read of her getting out of her place anymore. You haven't received a "whipping" until you have had one from God. Miriam started out to be a real helper but she became a hinderer when she let pride and jealousy come into her heart. These two sins will rob Christians of their humble, sincere service to God. Poor Miriam! She found this out but she had to find it out the hard way.

Many people believe that their name is all they have and if you mess up their name they are doomed. Well your reputation is the same way. However, people can talk about you and not really know you which creates a false illusion as to who you really are. Some folks are defined by their occupations, and that's clearly the case with **Rahab.** Truth is, her job was practically her last name, Rahab-the-Harlot. Yes, Rahab was what many of us refer to as a "street walker" or a "lady of the night." Rahab was a business owner. She was an innkeeper in the city of Jericho. In about 1400 B.C., when the Israelites invaded Canaan, Rahab hid three Hebrew spies. Her conviction that God was real led her to ask that she and her family would be preserved when Jericho fell. The mere plan of Joshua to send spies in to survey the Promised Land created a change in the life of a woman through a conversation. We call that today "witnessing." These two spies through God's guidance made their way there seeking help. She recognized them as God's men, and upon hearing that the king was seeking them; she had that needed wisdom to hide them upon the roof of her house. Rahab told them during her conversation that she knew that her city was to fall to Joshua's army; and how she had heard of God's miracle of drying up the Red Sea. The king of Jericho knew that Rahab's house is most likely where the spies would go, since she was the innkeeper. And it was told that the king of Jericho, said, "Behold there are men in hither tonight of the children of Israel to search out the country" (Joshua 2:2). It is amazing how people think they know you like that and can "yank" your chain. So the king of Jericho sent this message to Rahab: "Bring out the men who came to you and entered your house, because they have come to spy out the whole land." (Joshua 2:3). Well, well, well was this a suggestion or command one would ask? Rahab was faced with a difficult choice, in every life story decisions are made in haste that determine the course of eternity. Rahab was only "Bad for a Season", but not forever..." Because of the decision Rahab made to send the militia police looking elsewhere and not give up the spies put her in a new category of bad girls. She had graduated to an ugly acting girl. Rahab had heard about God and unlike the others in Jericho she chose to acknowledge and trust him. She was also a woman devoted to her family, when she struck a deal to protect the spies she asked for protection not just for herself but her family as well. Rahab reminds believers not to be judgmental. All have sinned, and if not for God's grace, all would be doomed. God extends us grace and we must extend grace to others. So can bad people that do ugly things still be blessed? Rahab, a wicked harlot, stepped in sin, who believed and trusted in God, and by doing so she became one of His saved children and blessed above her expectations.

It is all in the family with **Tamar.** She was fortunate to have been married to two brothers who both died and then their father fathered her children. Wow! It sounds like a soap opera. So what is the background of acting "ugly" with Tamar? Her story has it all: mysterious deaths, deceptive relatives, mistaken identities, hidden babies, even a woman sentenced to burn at the stake! Tamar means "palm tree". When Judah's wicked son Er died, leaving his widow Tamar childless, Judah gave his son Onan to her so she would be able to have a child. The story goes on to tell how Onan refused to let his semen spill in Tamar so he had it spill on the ground because he had issues about the child being an heir to his dead brother Er. He too soon died for disobedience. Well the story continues with Judah making a promise to Tamar that when the third son was of age he would be given to her in marriage. Well it didn't happen. So in time, Judah's wife died and after his period of mourning had passed, Tamar learned that he would be traveling to Timnah. She covered her face with a veil and posed as a prostitute at a point on Judah's route. How tricky, scheming, and deceitful can a woman be?

You know payback can be ugly. Realizing Judah would never honor the levirate law, Tamar took matters into her own hands. She was more concerned with being a mother than with being, good, so she devised a plan. Finally, Tamar "took off her widow's garments" and posed as a prostitute by the side of the road Judah frequented. Judah, assuming she was a harlot, had sex with her and left his signet and staff with her as a pledge until he could send a lamb to pay the price she demanded. When he left her, Tamar returned to Judah's camp with Judah's signet and staff. So what is a woman to do when the monthly menstruation doesn't show up and she begins to panic? The word gets out that she is pregnant and customs say that Judah is to condemn her. But Tamar comes clean and shares who the father is. When Judah realized that he had denied her justice under levirate law, he could only say, "She has been more righteous than I" (Gen. 38:26). In addition Tamar had the signet and staff as proof of her accusation. Judah rescinded her death sentence. Tamar gave birth to twin boys, Perez and Zerah. Perez was in the direct line of the ancestry of David, and thus the line of Jesus. Sometimes a woman has got to do what she has to do even if it is ugly.

There are some additional ugly women in the Bible and the few listed prior were Leah, Miriam and Rahab. Other women to consider are Lot's wife and Job's wife. What's with these Godly men having these *ugly wives*. Let's talk about **Lot's wife**. The angels had warned the family members not to look back when Sodom and the cities of the plain were destroyed. Lot's wife disobeyed and was "turned into a pillar of salt." Women that are married to decision makers or authority heads have a role to play as a listener. The story of Lot's wife is an example of poor communication in a family and how it causes you to act ugly. When Abraham had renegotiated with the Angels to spare the city if they could find 10 good people, they went on to Sodom and Gomorrah where Lot saw them and invited them into the house. The wicked people saw the two men who were angels go into the house and they told Lot to send them out. The wicked people started acting a fool trying to break down the door, when the power of the angels blinded them they backed off. The two men said to Lot, "Do you have anyone else here, sons-in-law, sons or daughter, or anyone else in the city who belongs to you?" (Genesis 19:12) . Well the to be sons-in-laws thought it was a joke and again the angels told Lot to hurry and just take your wife and daughters, even though they didn't have enough to make the ten. At this point Lot has not talked to, or

37

should I say not communicated to his wife on what is happening. Lot hurried with his wife and daughters, and the angels kept giving directions, on what to do and they even gave specific directions once they cleared the city gates. The Scriptures say: "And it came to pass, when they had brought them forth abroad, that he said, escape for they life; look not behind thee, neither stay though in all the plain; escape to the mountain; lest thou be consumed." (Genesis 19:17). The angels were telling Lot and his family not to look back. In the background the cracking and popping of fire was happening. All of a sudden Lot's wife looked back. She was behind her husband all along, remember. Perhaps she was lingering even farther back than necessary. The sounds of destruction and horror must have been deafening and frightening. But his wife from behind him looked back. Why did she look back? That's what stumped scholars for centuries. It's this one mistake that made her a bad girl. It's what earned her a place in Scripture, both Old Testament and New. It's what killed her too. Just down right disobedience and hard-headed, just won't follow directions, challenging authority with non-verbal behavior these are all adjectives describing *ugly acting* with Lot's wife.

Another wife that acted ugly but verbalized it was **Job's wife**. When a family member is suffering and you feel for them but that crazy mouth just opens up and some of the most ignorant things depart from it, as with Job's wife. Here this man had been suffering with boils all over his body so she saw no relationship with him. She is mentioned only after Job had lost his wealth and his children along with "painful boils from the soles of his feet to the crown of his head" (Job 2:7). As Job sat in ashes, exhausted and in pain, his wife spoke, " Do you still hold fast to your integrity? Curse God and die!" But he said to her, "You speak as one of the foolish women speaks. Shall we indeed accept good from God, and shall we not accept adversity?" (Job 2:9-10). When individuals are sick like Job and your friends are putting you down and asking questions as to why this is happening to you, it would really help if your spouse had "your back" and was there to give support. But Job's wife like so many women when your spouse or family member is down they will leave you in a hurry. Some women just can't take the pain and suffering they see before them. With Job's wife she was losing everything around her and when things start happening and we refer to them as (*in 3's*) you can't help but notice and she had to say something. She had lost children, cattle and servants. She was distraught and felt victimized and her faith wasn't as strong as Job's. Job's wife was quite human, and she displayed a natural response to human suffering. But Job's response was Godly and showed spiritual depth. We need always to check our reactions, for they may well be carnal rather than spiritual.

Mrs. Job was not a cold, uncaring faithless woman. She was a woman who understood suffering and pain. She was a woman who thought about her situation and tried to see the options available to her. She was a woman who pushed us to think about who we are and whose we are-really. Thank God that Mrs. Job was brave enough to speak up!

Study Notes

CHAPTER 2

JESUS' RELATIONSHIP WITH WOMEN

It is amazing how the relationship that Jesus had with women was so phenomenal. Jesus is shown exalting women far above the limited positions they were granted in the first-century Jewish world. Women were filled with the Holy Spirit and privileged to prophesy. Women were welcomed as learners and disciples. Jesus served as a son, a brother, a father and a best friend. Each relationship that he had is defined by the following women and each of their names' was Mary.

We Are Family

Mary, the mother of Jesus, had the most profound opportunity any woman could imagine, she gave birth to Jesus. During her engagement, Mary was visited at her home in Nazareth by the Angel Gabriel, who said to her, "Greeting favored one! The Lord is with you" (Luke 1:28).

Can you imagine what had to be going through her mind at that time? She was the first to hear that God was about to break into history in the person of the Messiah, her son-to-be, and Mary was the first to hear His name, Jesus. Mary stands apart from all women in history. She never claimed anything for herself, but adoration of her is ageless, classless, race less and timeless. I think of the announcement to Mary and what could have been going through her mind because Joseph surely had to question what is this? Scripture reveals to us that God took care of the issues or questions that Joseph encountered. Like many mothers, Mary saw Jesus grow into a young man. As a young boy just entering adulthood, Jesus was separated from his parents at the temple. After a frantic search, they found him, and Mary mildly scolded him for allowing them to be worried. He replied, with what appears to be genuine amazement, "Why did you seek me? Did you not know that I must be about my Father's business? (Luke 2:49). Another encounter that Mary plays a vital role was the first miracle. Mary was present at Jesus' first miracle when he changed the water to wine at a wedding in Cana In fact, she prompted the miracle by telling Jesus that the supply of wine was exhausted and then telling the servants to obey Jesus' commands.

The third time the scripture gives her appearance was at the cross. This was the climax of all Mary's heartache and sorrow. Mary, like so many mothers, worried and hurt when people talked about Jesus negatively and criticizing him for being different. She was an extraordinary woman of God and we were so blessed to have her as the surrogate mother of our Savior and Lord.

The **sorrowing woman** is a story in the Bible where a widow who has lost her only son is on his way to be buried. The birth of this son had been an occasion for great celebration. In the Jewish culture, giving birth to a son gave a woman value in her husband's eyes. A baby boy ensured the hope of passing on the family wealth and name. His presence was guaranteed social security. It would be his responsibility to care for his aging parents, and especially for his widowed mother.

Jesus and the disciples climbed up a hill and could see a processional of people mourning, shrieking and crying. Jesus had reached the top of the hill and he came down to walk beside the widow who was crying and he started talking to her telling her not to cry. And he came and touched the bier; and they that bare him stood still. And he said, 'Young man, I say unto thee, arise! (Luke 7:14) .

Jesus showed compassion to the woman. The sweetest words can and need to be shared with women when they are grieving. Jesus saying to the woman "weep not" were some of the most comforting words one could want to hear. There was the side of Jesus that he showed when he needed to and who he needed to show it to.

Female Friends

Having female friends was an important attribute that Jesus possessed. Most of his male friends had either sisters or mothers that Jesus cared about. One such person was **Mary the mother of John Mark**. Mary had an open door policy for prayer. Mary's home served as a place of worship for part of the Christian community in Jerusalem. She evidently was a woman of some wealth, for she not only owned a house big enough to accommodate a large group, but she also had servants. Though the Bible does not say, tradition holds that Mary's home was also the place where the last supper was served and where the apostles and a group of women met and prayed following Jesus ascension.

Mary lived with her brother Lazarus and her sister Martha. They were all close friends of Jesus and others opened their homes to him as he traveled through Bethany. Mary preferred sitting at Jesus' feet listening to what he said. There were several encounters where Mary showed her love for Jesus as a sister would to a brother in Christ. She acted out when her brother Lazarus had died and she expected Jesus to do something about it. Then when she poured the expensive perfume on his feet everyone thought she had lost her mind. However, Jesus knew that this would be his final trip to Jerusalem. His closest friends seemed oblivious to the confrontation sure to come to-all of his friends, that is, except Mary. She saw the significance of what was happening. Mary demonstrated her awareness of the events about to unfold, as well as her devotion to Jesus, by one extraordinary act. Friends are there when you need them and Mary and Jesus were truly family since they were like brother and sister.

Mary, mother of James and Joses and probably the wife of Clopas, is referred to in the Scriptures as "the other Mary." This Mary was present at Jesus' crucifixion, and stood near his cross with Jesus' mother, sister and Mary Magdalene. This proves that Jesus had many women in his life that shared the name Mary. Mary was a common name in the first century which was shared by many of the women Jesus knew.

Another woman, the **suffering woman** stood out to Jesus literally. Everybody knows about the woman with the issue of blood, but for those who don't know this is the background information. There was an unnamed woman who had suffered for twelve long years going back and forth to doctors trying to find out what was wrong with her. She may have taken ground-up willow bark to try to reduce her pain. This was a bitter tasting remedy containing salicin, an aspirin-like drug that would have only aggravated her bleeding. In those days a woman having a disease such as hers was considered unclean and she was not to be around other people let alone touch anyone.

This woman had heard of the miracles that Jesus was doing, how he was healing the sick, the paralyzed and raising people from the dead. She had heard about the powerful words that he used when he did these miracles.

This woman saw Jesus on his way to see about Jairus' daughter and she thought to herself, "If I could just touch the hem of his garment I will be made whole." There were so many people pressing, pushing and shoving trying to get a glimpse as well as touch Jesus. Keeping her face down to avoid being recognized, she waded out into the sweating mass of people following him.

Persistently, she worked her way deeper into the tight circle surrounding Him until finally she was near enough to touch Him. She reached out and lightly touched His garment for just an instant.

Immediately her bleeding stopped. And Jesus immediately knowing in himself that virtue had gone out of him, turned him about in the press, and said, 'Who touched my clothes'? I'm healed! I'm healed! You talk about some screaming and shouting a Holy Ghost party was in the making, it was a celebration. She hadn't touched his skin, only the hem of his garment, how could Jesus have discerned it? Such is the mystery of a miracle. He hadn't felt her presence in His body; he felt it with his Spirit, for "a touch of faith could not be hidden from Him".

What a man, what a man, what a man, what a mighty, mighty, good man. As women who have been sick and having issues of blood and other medical disorders, we know what she was going through. Thank you, Lord for medical technology. But this woman had Jesus, Jesus the most powerful healer. This was Dr. J-E-S-U-S, the one who can speak and pain will disappear. Thank you, Jesus for the compassion shown to the women with illnesses.

The **woman caught in adultery also known as the adulteress woman** had a personal relationship with Jesus and how they met was really interesting. This woman is one of many unnamed persons in the Gospels who are known by their condition or sin. She is the woman caught in adultery. This woman has no name and very little voice. Yet she plays an important role in helping us to understand Jesus and the powers over against which he stood. Here is the background of the story. Jesus is at the temple teaching everybody and the Scribes and Pharisees interrupt his lesson. They are dragging a woman that they caught in the act of committing adultery. They have her stand in front of Jesus and they ask Jesus a question. They say unto him, master, this woman was taken into adultery; in the very act. Now Moses' in the law commanded us, that such should be stoned: but what sayest thou? (John 8:4-5). Now at this point Jesus knows that they are testing him to see how he will respond. So he slowly stooped down and with his finger he wrote in the dirt and he was acting like he hadn't heard them. So they kept on asking him and he finally stood up and said "He that is without sin among you, let him first cast a stone at her." (John 8:7).

Jesus was so cool that he just stooped back down and kept writing in the dirt. In the meantime the woman is silent. We can only imagine what she must have been feeling. She stands before the great teacher who has a reputation of forgiving sins and making people, even women, feel important and valuable. "When they heard it, they went away, one by one, beginning with the elders; and Jesus was left alone with the woman standing before Him. Jesus straightened up and said to her 'Woman, where are they? Has no one condemned you?' She said, "No one, sir..' And Jesus said, 'Neither do I condemn you. Go your way, and from now on do not sin again'" (John 8:9-11).

Yes! Thank you, Jesus what a man. Lord, have mercy on all women who commit adultery or have committed adultery. Women are forgiven and he asks that we sin no more. Thank you, Jesus for the compassion shown to this woman. The law stated that she was to be stoned and Lord Jesus you stepped in and no stone was thrown. Thank you, Lord for compassion that was shown to the woman while the Scribes and Pharisees "used" her to try and test Jesus. Thank you, Lord for Jesus having a discerning spirit of forgiveness. May all women who have been adulterers, caught up in adultery or contemplating an affair realize that Jesus can fix it if you only ask.

<u>Dealing with the Enemy</u>

It is interesting to note that with all the Marys' that Jesus had encounters with; this one is the most noted for her personal relationship with Jesus. As Jesus and his disciples traveled from town to town, a group of exceptional women followed and supported them wherever they went. **Mary Magdalene** was among these women. What made Mary Magdalene feel so indebted to Jesus and to follow him around from place to place? Curiosity was tempting me to find out why. Mary Magdalene was a woman whose life had been transformed by Jesus. He had delivered her from seven demons that dominated her. She was dealing with the enemy internally. We can surmise the depth of her gratitude by her commitment to Jesus that she showed afterward. Mary dedicated herself to Jesus and His cause. She contributed funds to help Jesus continue preaching and teaching.

Friends will be there for you when you need them most and so it was no surprise that Mary Magdalene was at the cross and observed Jesus endure this cruel method of Roman execution, and witness his burial. She saw the Romans roll an enormous stone in front of the tomb where Jesus was laid. Mary Magdalene was still hanging around when the stone was rolled away and the two angels inside asked her why was she crying. The relationship with Jesus was special because when she saw the Gardner she asked him, "Where did they lay Jesus' body?" But when Jesus spoke her name, Mary recognized his voice and called him Rabboni, meaning my teacher. Friends, real friends, best of friends, is what Jesus was to Mary Magdalene.

A mother caring for her children experiences stress, strain, heartaches and fear when something happens to them. But to know that you can call on Jesus and to have what we call a **mother's faith** takes you to another level. This story is about a miracle that Jesus performed (it sounds like a magic show) to let the people of Galilee see the power of God. When Jesus performed his miracles he always had a lesson to be taught behind it. When Jesus and the disciples were on their way to Galilee they were close to the areas where the Syrophenician people lived.

You have heard of the Hatfields and the McCoys in the westerns, always fighting. Well, the Syrophecians and Israelites were similar to the Hatfields and McCoys. They hated each other and were attacking each other all the time. Jesus was not and has not ever been about "mess" he has always wanted everyone to get along. So this particular day as they were walking, a woman came up to him and asked for help. The woman told Jesus that a demon had taken over her daughter's body. Jesus knew this woman was a Syrophecian and he was an Israelite, so he put her to the test by saying: "I am not sent but unto the lost sheep of the house of Israel" (Matthew 18:7). By this he was asking her, Shouldn't I help my own people first? Jesus said that taking away from his people's needs to help a Syrophecian is absurd. But this "gutsy" Syrophecian woman, looked Jesus straight in the eyes and said, "Truth Lord: yet dogs eat of the crumbs which fall from their masters table." Then Jesus answered and said unto her, "O woman great is thy faith: be it unto thee even as thou wilt." And the story goes on to say that her daughter was made whole from that very hour. So why did this woman approach Jesus as she did? She might have no right to appeal to Him on the basis of a covenant relationship, but she could and did appeal to Him as a needy creature, who recognized that as God there was no limit to Jesus' ability to meet every human need.

Yes! Yes! Yes! I've been there! Done that! I have the receipts to show for it. God has brought many a mother through the heartaches and headaches that our children have put us through. It has taken faith in God to know that you will get the money to get them out of jail. You will be able to get the right lawyer to take the case with things your child has been involved in. You will be able to get the diagnoses confirmed on the test results from the right doctor. All of these things are relative to having or should we say *keeping the faith*. We know and trust that the banker is Jesus, the lawyer or attorney is Jesus and the doctor is Dr. Jesus and that they are all in one. As women we need to believe in the Scripture that says "If you have the faith of a mustard seed you shall say to the mountain 'move' and it will move." So don't you know that if you have faith in God, he is going to make it happen? There is nothing that is to hard for God, all we have to do is have the faith and he will take it from there.

CHAPTER 3

WOMEN OF THEN AND NOW

There are women from all walks of life that make up the Christian family. All have not always been saved. We are experiencing a vast amount of women who have to go out make the money to buy the bacon and come home and cook it. The women over 2,000 years ago tended the cattle, slaughtered it and prepared it for serving. So things have not changed, if you want to know why something is happening now search the word and you will find it in the Bible. This next section deals with biblical women and their occupations.

Professions of Women

Fancy titles and occupations of merit are fine to have but what you do with the monies received for your work is really important. When women have the opportunity to give they give believing that the more you give, the more He'll give to you. He, meaning God. With the parable of the **poor widow**, again Luke chose to tell the story of a woman chosen from the lowest strata of society, and again her actions showed that what she could contribute was extremely significant to the Lord. Christ's commendation once again marks a striking reversal of status. The great gifts given by wealthy men were dismissed, while the tiny gift given by the widow was commended as "more than all" (Luke 21:3).

Worker and Homemaker

Martha, the sister of Mary and Lazarus, always served as hostess at family gatherings. Jesus had apparently come at Martha's invitation. She was the one who welcomed Him in, signifying that she was the actual master of ceremonies in this house. Even her name is the feminine form of the Aramaic word for "Lord." It was a perfect name for her because she was clearly the one who presided over the house.

Often times we are given roles and people will categorize us because they think those are the only skills we have. Martha not only accepted society's view of her role; she became upset when her sister Mary did not help her. Martha's agitation is not so much a reflection of her need for kitchen help as it is anxiety at Mary's "inappropriate" behavior! Jesus had a way of getting or should I say getting things straightened out. He stepped in just like a big brother and put Martha in her place. Jesus gave Martha a mild rebuke and a strong lesson about where her real priorities ought to lie. And Jesus answered and said to her, "Martha, Martha, you are worried and troubled about many things, but one thing is needed, and Mary has chosen that good part, which will not be taken away from her" (Luke 10:42). Martha's external behavior at first appeared to be true servanthood. She was the one who put on the apron and went to work on the task of serving others. However, she was a real friend to Jesus and she was just like a sister and his scolding her was truly in love.

Another working woman story is about the **Woman and Elijah**. When Elijah had left the wilderness God was sending ravens with food and he got thirsty so he drank from a brook. There was no rain and Elijah had to travel because the brook had dried up. While he was traveling he came to a woman's house and asked for food and water.

She told him she had only enough flour to make one last meal before she and her son would be starved to death. Elijah told her he was a prophet and that God had sent him. He told her God will provide. This woman believed him and she did as he instructed. Sure enough, the woman made meal after meal and the same amount of flour was "stretching." This was a miracle. Yes! Lord, you know how to provide for women when we don't know where the next meal is going to come from or how we are going to feed or make lunches for the children, but you do provide - that's God. Yes! He used Elijah to perform the miracle, but that's God providing all that she needed. God will provide for you if only you ask and when you ask, ask boldly, trusting and believing that he will come through.

Deborah was a hard working woman and how she got her position is even more extraordinary. The first thing we learn of Deborah is that she had a special relationship with God. She had been called by Him and commissioned to speak in His name.

She was a prophetess and a "leader of Israel." But Deborah was also a wife, a member of Lepidoth's household. There was no essential conflict between being a wife in a patriarchal age and being a spiritual leader. Deborah was a working woman. She was considered one of Israel's great judges and the only woman on record to hold this position of leadership over Israel

Deborah was often found sitting under a palm tree between Bethel and Ramah. And Israelites from various tribes would consult her to settle their disputes. The most noted victory for Deborah was giving direction to Barak on fighting a war that God had given her directions to give to Barak. The outcome is phenomenal. Deborah was a woman whose confidence was rooted in a close personal relationship with God and in her awareness that God had chosen to use her to guide His people.

Deborah reminds us that God does gift women for spiritual leadership. We do violence to scripture if we rule women out of leadership solely on the basis of gender. At the same time, God's choice of Barak as military commander may indicate that not every leadership role is appropriate for women.

Anna was a prophetess not a preacher. A prophetess is one who speaks in the power of the Holy Spirit. God commands women to keep silence in the church not to usurp authority over man. So a prophetess witnessed to individuals and never to mixed congregations. So how can we describe Anna's role as a prophetess? Anna may have been a teacher of the Old Testament to other women. She is nonetheless called a prophetess because it was her habit to declare the truth of God's word to others. This gift for proclaiming God's truth ultimately played a major role in the ministry, for which Anna is still best remembered. Anna who had dedicated her life to serve God in the temple, not only recognized the babe in Mary's arms, but proclaimed Him to "all those who looked for redemption in Jerusalem." Anna was truly rewarded by seeing the Christ child while serving the Lord in the temple.

Enterprising and Entrepreneur

Lydia was the first convert in Macedonia. Her occupation as a seller of purple cloth and later sponsoring of Paul and the Philipian Church in her own home indicates that she was both wealthy and influential. Lydia was a true business woman and entrepreneur. When she settled in Philipi in Macedonia, there she could market her expensive purple cloth among the social elite, military retirees, and ruling families.

When she heard the apostle Paul speak in the business district at Phillipi, she reaffirmed the decision she had made earlier to convert to Judaism and worship God alone.

Once you get saved things happen for the good and you know that it is all God. Not much is said of Lydia in the scriptures but from her we learn that salvation comes to anyone who will accept it and that one can be in business and still be a Christian and serve the Lord.

The **Nobles Wife** is described to many of us through Proverbs 31 and is also known as the **Virtuous Woman**. It proves that it's okay to work outside the home. In our day we are familiar with stereotypes that too often are used to determine appropriate male and female roles. Women and men with their work ethics have been compared as well. We assume a woman is more nurturing and is the appropriate person to care for children. So men should work outside the home, and women should work at home. Women are verbal, so they make good teachers and social workers. Stereotypes, stereotypes, will we ever get away from them? For many Christians, these notions are justified by what they suppose the Bible teaches even though proof texts are hard to find.

The **woman who came to Elisha** for help is a prime example of just asking how it can be beneficial. The woman told Elisha her situation about the man who her husband owed some money and he was about to take her sons as slaves. This woman needed some help and some finances very quick. Elisha, asked the woman did she have any food in her house and woman responded all I have is this one little bowl of olive oil. Elisha told her to collect as many containers, bowls, pots and jars as she could. He even told her to borrow some if she had to. Then Elisha told her to fill all the containers, pots, jars, and bowls from the little bowl. She started filling the containers, pots, bowls and jars and there was enough to sell and pay back the man all the money her deceased husband had borrowed. This was a miracle. Isn't God good! So many times women are faced with decisions of what to do and wham! God performs a miracle. He is so good his wonders never cease to amaze me.

Witness and Missionary

There has always been and will be an opportunity to witness and worship. You may serve as a witness or missionary. This either by telling your personal testimony or going forth and spreading the word about what God has done for you.

The **women disciples** were the "groupies" that hung around the disciples. Without laboring the point, the first mention in Acts of women pictures them gathered with men, for prayer and worship,. This scene alone indicates that the new freedom Christ offered by those who trusted in Him. The women who witnessed the resurrection and critics have also pointed to variations in the accounts of Jesus' resurrection in the gospels, such as how many women came into the tomb and who they were.

We have got to get past the roles of gender when it comes to being a witness and a missionary. God always had a way to speak to the women. The angels in reminding the women of Jesus' words made it clear that these women were disciples who had been taught by Christ just as the twelve had been taught. Jesus had taught the women the same truths He taught the men. Their gender and even their willingness to do "women's work" in no way limited their status to Christ's disciples!

God provides for women through jobs, positions, titles, but how we share the word with others is on us. We can be a witness and missionary everyday. I consider the **woman at the well** as one of the most unique marketing tools around because she used "word of mouth" to tell her story. She was a *true* witness.

The Pharisees heard that Jesus was making more believers and baptizing more than John was. Jesus knew the Pharisees were watching him so he decided to leave Judea and go to Galilee, but he had to pass through Samaria in order to get there. When Jesus got to the small town of Sychar he stopped at Jacob's well because he was thirsty. He looks down the road and a woman is coming with her pots and this is strange because women don't come in the noon day, they come in the evening when it is cooler. Jesus asked the woman for a drink of water. She responded to him that she was surprised that he asked her for a drink. She stated, "You are a Jew and I am a Samaritan." Jesus told her, "You don't know what God gives. And you don't know who asked you for a drink. If you knew, you would have asked me, and I would have given you living water." She immediately understood that He was making an amazing claim. She replied, "Sir, you have nothing to draw with, and the well is deep. Where then do you get that living water? Are you greater than our father Jacob, who gave us the well, and drank from it himself, as well as his sons and his livestock?"(John 4:11-12).

Jesus told her that every person who drinks this water will be thirsty again.

"But whosoever drinketh of the water that I shall give him shall never thirst; but the water that I shall give him shall be in him a well of water springing up into everlasting life" (John 4:14).

Now she was supremely curious, and she asked Him to give her the living water. I think by now she probably understood that He was speaking of spiritual water. Jesus' next words unexpectedly drew her up short: "Go, call your husband, and come here.". Wow! This had to have blown her away but she gathered her wits about her and responded to Jesus. "I have no husband," she replied (John 4:17). Jesus said to her, "You are right when you say you have no husband, and the man you now have is not your husband." (John 4:18). Tell it! Tell it! Tell it! You know her heart had to be sinking; Jesus had just called her out. Jesus reaffirmed to her stating that she had no husband was true, and she never said she didn't deny that she had had five husbands nor did she say anything about the man she was living with. What she did say to Jesus was that she could see he was a prophet. They went on to have their discussions about Samaritan and Jewish worship. She replied with these amazing words: "I know that Messiah is coming (who is called Christ). 'When he comes, He will tell us all things'"(John 4: 25).

No sooner had she broached the subject of the Messiah, then Jesus said, " I who speak to you am He" (John 4:26). This is the single most direct and explicit messianic claim Jesus ever made. Never before in any of the biblical record had He said this so forth rightly to anyone . So what do you say or do after receiving a response from Jesus like this? Her response was typical of new believers, one of the evidences of authentic faith. The person who has just had the burden of sin and guilt lifted always wants to share the good news with others. The woman's excitement would have been palpable. And notice that the first thing she told the men of her town was that Jesus had told her everything she ever did. No longer was she evading the facts of her sin. She was basking in the glow of forgiveness, and there is simply no shame in that.

The woman at the well didn't wait for a door to swing open; she kicked it down herself. I have to repeat this again, "Come, see a man who told me everything I ever did." Why did the men of her city listen to her, a woman with a shady lifestyle? Simple; She had seen the Christ. Now the people of Sychar saw the Christ in her. A changed life gets people's attention every time.

This is the most compelling woman to me, because she is so real. She doesn't put on a front and pretend to be something she is not. Jesus called her out and she is not ashamed of it. She only asked for the water that is going to change her forever. We all need to get some of the water. We as women need to let it flow down through our body and cleanse us of all the dirt, sin, hatred, and pettiness that exists. Thank God for the woman at the well so women can see that if she can tell it why can't we. Don't hold back when he has blessed you. You ought to tell it! Women don't be ashamed of your past tell it! Tell it! Tell it! Tell it! Tell it! The Lord wants to use everyday women, the real women, the women who trust, the women who have faith, the women who believe, and the women that won't give up! Tell it! Tell it! Tell it! Be a witness!

The women who washed Jesus feet, Mary the sister of Martha and Lazarus was one, but there was another. They both are prime examples of the women who cared for Jesus. Jesus was in the midst of having a meal with the Pharisees and he knew that they did not trust him, but every opportunity he got he taught a lesson. This particular time that they were sitting down to eat. "There came unto Him a woman having an alabaster box of very precious ointment and poured it on his head."(Matthew 26:7).

Alabaster was a soft stone, imported from Egypt into Palestine, especially popular for storing perfume and ointments. It was light and creamy in color, usually faintly lined with veins. It was pint-size, palm size, purse size. Alabaster jars were common, it was the substance hidden that was valuable. It contained all the perfume the woman owned. The tiniest dab of perfume on the appropriate pulse points lasted well into the dark desert night.

After pouring the perfume on his head she knelt down behind him. She was crying and as the tears fell from her eyes they mixed with the perfume as she poured it on Jesus' dusty feet. She then wiped the perfume from his feet with her hair and then kissed his feet while she is still crying again and again. Meanwhile Simon the Pharisee is looking down at the woman and thinking to himself, "If Jesus was a prophet, He wouldn't have her doing this." She knew what the townsfolk thought of her. Their whispered words and rude stares made that painfully clear. But this Jesus was different. His words were kind, not cruel. His gaze reflected compassion, not judgment. Thought of such a man looking at her surely had her trembling with expectation.

In the book of Matthew the story continues with Jesus calling Simon the Pharisee out since he was talking to himself, remember Jesus knows all things, and Jesus tells him the story of the creditor and the debtor. The disciples started getting attitudes and wanted to know why she would do something like this. "For this ointment might have been sold for much, and given to the poor." (Matthew 26:9).

Ignoring the disciples Jesus continued teaching his lesson to Simon the Pharisee. "Do you see this woman?"(Luke 7:44) "See her," Jesus implored. "See her as I see her. I came into your house. You did not give me any water for my feet, but she wet my feet with her tears and wiped them with her hair." (Luke 7:44) "You did not give me a kiss, but this woman, from the time I entered, has not stopped kissing my feet." (Luke 7:45) "You did not put oil on my head, but she has poured perfume on my feet." (Luke 7:46). By pointing out the things she did right and the things Simon should have done, Jesus managed to affirm her and admonish him at the same time, without stripping either one of dignity. Lord, Lord, Lord thank you for forgiveness. Just knowing that he knows what we have done as women and everyone else wants to keep reminding us of "what" we used to do and to know that you forgive us and that can move on is so gracious, loving and kind.

Worship is about rekindling an ashen heart into a blazing fire. This woman was a torch bearer. Jesus surely felt the heat in her touch, her tears, and her kiss. She came asking for nothing, concerned only with giving him glory, honor, and praise the only way she knew how. Jesus said to the woman, " Your faith has saved you…" (Luke 7:50).

Deaconesses

There are often positions held in various church denominations for men and women. In the Baptist church you will have men and now women who are called deacons and other women who are called deaconess. In the Methodist church these positions are steward and stewardess. With their roles in both of these denominations comes the responsibilities of "doing good works." The people in these positions are responsible for caring for the sick, needy, the poor and down-trodden. They assist the church Pastor and attend to the needs of members of the church as well as the community. So it is all worth defining, **Tabitha** as one of the greatest deaconess in the Bible. The fascinating thing about this person is that she had the alias name of **Dorcas**. Dorcas was dearly loved in her church. She wasn't famous as a prophetess neither was she a preacher. Instead she was a woman full of good works and charitable deeds.

The people loved Dorcas because she cared for others and demonstrated her caring in practical ways.

So when this woman of good works became ill and died it affected an entire community and they sent for help. The disciples sent two men to get Peter who upon his arrival, was taken to an upstairs room where the body lay attended by mourners. Peter asked them to leave the room, and then, down on his knees praying, he told Tabitha to get up. She opened her eyes and sat up. News of the miracle spread quickly and prompted a great many people to accept Peter's teachings of the Gospel.[95] It is important to understand how the good you do for others while serving in the role of a deaconess or stewardess is history from Tabitha, also known as "Dorcas" and it should be an honor to serve others.

Phoebe/Phebe falls under the category as a deaconess. The word that describes her as a "servant" of the church could be translated "deaconess." So what set Phoebe apart from other women during this time with Paul? Phebe was probably a lady of means and social standing. She was a devoted and dedicated Christian and a member of the Church of Cenchera. Paul chose her to bear this epistle because of her trustworthiness and because she was going to Rome on business anyway.

So, at the end of Paul's letter to the Church at Rome, he recommended Phoebe to them and asked them to welcome her in the Lord when she came to their church. This was such an honor for a woman to be endorsed as a servant "deaconess" for the Lord.

As a leader of the church women have to be especially careful when they are in charge of monies even relative to ministries. The story of **Sapphira** and Ananias is one that the financial side of women should be reviewed and examined for flaws. Sapphira and Ananias are members of the early Christian church at Jerusalem. They are struck dead for withholding monies from the common fund. The members of the Christian church at Jerusalem had decided to pool their resources for the common good. The people sold their properties and contributed the proceeds to a common fund, which the apostles administered. This arrangement symbolized the utopian Israelite community where things were shared: "There will, however, be no one in need among you, because God is sure to bless you in the land that your God is giving you as a possession to occupy, if only you will obey your God by diligently observing this entire commandment that I command you today" (Deut. 15:4-5).

Sapphira and Ananias were clearly well-known among the believers. Perhaps they served in some leadership capacity for the young church, side by side as husband and wife, or had a thriving business that provided plenty of disposable income to support the cause. Whatever the scenario, two truths stand out: (1) They were followers of Christ; and (2) They had the means to further His kingdom in a significant way. At first blush, Sapphira was a *Good girl*, not a *Bad one*. But while others were filled with the Holy Spirit's power, they were emptied by their own jealousy and need for prestige and recognition.

The real scoop on the story is Sapphira and Ananias were selling off the land and not giving all the proceeds to the common fund, they were holding back some for themselves. Brother Peter being the good disciple that he was questioned Ananias about what he was doing. The Scripture says: But Peter said, "'Ananias, why hath Satan filled thine heart to lie to the Holy Ghost, and to keep back *part* of the price of the land?" (Acts 5:3). Now what could Ananias say to that, he has been caught and he has no where to go, so just come clean, but does he? By the time Peter got through giving him the third degree on messing with God's finances, Ananias just fell dead. Peter had some men come in and carry Ananias out.

After an interval of about three hours his wife came in, not knowing what had happened. Peter said to her, "Tell me whether you and your husband sold the land for such a price." And she said, "Yes, that was the price." Then Peter said to her, "How is it that you have agreed together to put the Spirit of God to the test? Look, the feet of those who have buried your husband are at the door, and they will carry you out." (Acts 5:7-9).

Sapphira suffers the same fate as her husband. Peter does not remind her that the land was hers to do with as she pleased. She is accused of conspiring with her husband to test the Spirit of God. "Immediately she fell down at his feet and died. When the young men came in they found her dead, so they carried her out and buried her beside her husband" (Acts 5:10). Alright now! Don't mess with God's fin ances. It isn't yours in the first place, he gives it to you and if you are not a good steward of it, he will take it away. There is a woman right now who is on trial for killing her husband who was a minister. The newspaper shared that the transcripts from the trial state the motive was finance related. The couple was caught in a scam of money fraud being used through various ministries. The wife was the financial partner and the husband had been on her about the disorganization and not keeping things up to date.

She stated that she only remembers going to the closet getting a shotgun and shooting him while he was in bed. She stated that he rolled over in the bed on to the floor and he asked her, why? She said all she could say to him was, "I'm sorry." This and many other stories like this are why women rebel, act out and kill. Women lose it temporarily when stress builds and they don't know what to do. We have shelters especially for women when they have been sexually assaulted, abused, neglected or homeless. Women can be the solid rock for the family, but when adversity comes and you don't have faith in God you will lose it. The conversations between husbands and wives who are leaders in the church often get tested with greed and misappropriation of funds. Women if you are in a leadership position and responsible for any type of monies relative to the church then you had better do the right thing. Don't get *caught up* in mess, chaos, confusion over the finances of the church. God will work it out just make sure that you are not stealing, borrowing or transacting fund transfers illegally. It will show up because God will have it revealed. The latest new wave of real estate that is being *caught* in the media are Christian real estate retreat centers, which are being sold, but have never actually existed. Women in the church get to know when and what your community funds are being used for and toward what.

CHAPTER 4

WOMEN AND THE WORD

It is amazing how much time women spend in the word of God. There are days as a woman that if I have not prayed, sung or read scripture that I feel a void. Women differ somewhat from men on how we pray, study and relate to church activities. It is through this chapter that I explore the tools needed for women to study and have a better prayer life. A questionnaire was designed as well to receive input from other women in this area. The women described throughout this chapter had prayed and it is revealed how their prayers were answered by God.

God Speaks to Women

When you hear or read of **Sarah/Saria**, Abraham's wife, what is the first thing you think of? Yes! "The old lady that had a baby at the age of ninety years old".

When compiling this information I wanted to characterize Sarah as one of the bad girls of the Bible. Her bad girl description would have been because she could throw fits and tantrums. She knew how to be manipulative. She could be impatient, temperamental, conniving, cantankerous, cruel, flighty, pouty, jealous, erratic, unreasonable, a whiner, a complainer, or a nag. By no means was she always the perfect model of godly grace and meekness.

Sarah is described as being a beautiful woman, in reading I found that at the age of sixty-five Abraham was concerned about other men looking at his wife because she was so preserved in beauty. Her beauty was admired and coveted by Abraham as well as the Egyptians. Abraham even tried to use Sarah's beauty to save his own life. She was not only a beautiful woman to look upon, but she had beauty within her heart and soul and held a position of favor in Abrahams' household. As with many of the Biblical women, Sarah was not feeling fulfilled because she had a void in that she was barren. As a woman Sarah looked for an opportunity to fulfill the promise made during marriage to bear Abraham children. So she let her maid Hagar sleep with her husband.

While we can certainly sympathize, even empathize with poor Saria in her deep sense of failure as a wife, the underlying principle means the same: she made a decision, and when it boomeranged on her, she shifted the blame to Abraham, refusing to accept responsibility. This sleeping thing was not all Sarah's doing because Abraham did participate. After the sleeping took place Sarah started treating Hagar just down right nasty and she still could not produce a child. She so badly wanted a child but her attitude and mistreatment eventually sent Hagar away. Hagar went out into the desert and had a little talk with God. God told Hagar to go back -- what an experience that was in the desert. When Hagar came back is when things changed for Abraham and Sarah including their names. Sarah changed after Hagar came back and she was 90 years old when the Lord told Abraham that she would bear a son. Sarah laughed when she heard this news, but in due time the child was born and named Isaac. The key to this information on Sarah is that God speaks through other people sometimes just to get to us. We need to always keep our eyes and ears ready to view and hear a spoken word.

Having your Shield and Armor

So often you will hear expressions of having your shield and armor, but what does this really mean? It means to be protected by the Holy Spirit when the enemy is on a war path to get you. We as women get so wrapped up in things of the world that we forget that there is a higher power that can destroy any evil that wants to engulf us. The enemy seems to come when you are walking closer and closer to God. So how is it that we as Christian women know how to recognize evil so that we can protect ourselves, and at the same time grow? "For many deceivers have gone out into the world who do not confess Jesus Christ as coming in the flesh. This is a deceiver and antichrist. Whoever transgresses and does not abide in the doctrine of Christ does not have God. He who abides in the doctrine of Christ has both the Father and the Son. If anyone comes to you and does not bring this doctrine, do not receive him into your house nor greet him; for he who greets him shares in his evil deeds (2 John 7, 9-11). When I am attacked by the enemy I know that God will protect me if only I ask. The greatest weapons are God's word, prayer, praise and worship. The word says to "submit to God. Resist the devil and he will flee from you" (James 4:7).

The devil hates it when we worship the Lord and it creates "The Battle". I have learned that the battle is not mine it's the Lord's. But there are ten things to do when you're in battle.

Ten Things to Do When You're in Battle

1. Stop everything and worship God.
2. Praise Him for already defeating your enemy.
3. Thank Him for fighting the battle for you.
4. Ask God if there is anything He wants you to do that you are not already doing.
5. Fast and Pray.
6. Declare your dependence upon Him.
7. Recognize that the battle is not yours but the Lord's.
8. Position yourself in the right place before God.
9. Refuse to have fear.
10. Quiet your soul in worship and watch God save you.

As I am writing this book the enemy is so strong on me he is pushing me to quit, stop, and give up. He is making excuses to keep me from writing. There are interferences with people who need help-- counseling has to be given to grieving people, and children doing unethical things. As the forces speak, I start calling out loud "Lord help me!" I'm scared, nervous that I won't make the deadline that I won't have enough words at the end of the book and all my work will be in vain. As I call out "Lord Help me!" I get reassurance from the Lord when he tells me to read what you just typed above. The Lord instructs us to put on the whole armor of God and "having done all", to stand strong (Ephesians 6:13). We stand strong against the forces, opposing us every time we worship God.

Lord I know that worship is our greatest weapon of warfare. When we praise God in the midst of an enemy attacking, his attack is weakened and he must flee. Lord thank you right now, I feel some relief. The adversary doesn't want me to praise you or tell others why I give you the praise. As for you, Lord, You are "a shield to all who trust" in you (Psalm 18:28-30). You deliver me from the enemy who is too strong for me (Psalm 18:17).

Daily Devotions

It is so fascinating to read the various books published for women that are relative to devotional studies. A questionnaire survey was taken to reveal from women of varying ages and races about their daily devotional habits. The sample letter of request and the questionnaire survey will be listed at the end of this section.

There are several books that give devotional scripture and a story that follows to enhance and support the scripture given on a daily basis. An excerpt from one of the women and why she uses the books states: "I was a woman in desperate need of *Simple Abundance*". While reviewing research information I noted on the Sarah Breathnach, Simple Abundance cover a testimonial." During this time of profound introspections, six practical, creative, and spiritual principles-gratitude, simplicity, order, harmony, beauty, and joy-became the catalysis that helped me define a life of my own. Feeling confident again, I proposed writing a downshift lifestyle book for women who want, as I do, to live by their own lights." There are books that list answers for your daily needs by category from *abandonment* to *worthiness* and supports each category with Scriptures. Sometimes it's hard to find answers just when we need them most.

The book *Touch Points* is a valuable tool for discovering what God says about Women's particular needs and circumstances. Each entry contains thought-provoking questions, answers from Scripture and a promise from God's word. There are monthly, bi-monthly and even six month daily devotional material available. The book, *God's Word for Simple Abundance*, will guide you along the way if you're a new or old devotion participant. There are six months worth of devotions (180 in all), that lead you through the ancient yet timely biblical book of Proverbs explaining its wisdom and offering insights for your life today. The *Daily Bread and The Upper Room* are probably the most noted and used forms of daily devotion materials. Many churches purchase these items for their congregations to use. While doing research I found in the March-April 2005, The Upper Room Devotion Guide an article about the celebration of the guide being 70 years old. It stated that over 70 years ago a group of women from Travis Park Methodist Church in San Antonio, Texas began seeking a way to live out Jesus' words from the Gospel of Mark. They believed families and individuals needed guidance to encourage a daily practice of reading scripture, praying, and sharing the faith journey. This group of women saw a need, considered how they could make a difference and subsequently planted a seed of faith. As a result of their

86

thoughtfulness, we have *The Upper Room daily devotional guide.* An insert from the book says: "When I look to see what resources of study Bibles individuals used I was surprised at one specifically for *Women of Color*, the King James Version." There were special notes and features created to strengthen the spirit and encourage the hearts of women of African descent. When I began to concentrate on specific portions of devotion like prayer there were devotional items that walked you step by step through what to do and how to do it. The *Listening Heart* is a daily devotional for women and by women. If God's voice sometimes seems silent, hushed by the business of your life, take a few moments each day to contemplate his love as demonstrated in the lives of other women like you. Writings from around the world, tell how they are learning to listen to His still small voice. Another great book for devotions is *Quiet Time an Intervarsity Guidebook for Daily Devotions;* this book explained what quiet time is all about. The secret of the successful Christian life undoubtedly lies in the quiet times which are those sacred moments of the day when the Christian communes with his Lord.

Being a woman of color I was surprised that when it came to prayer that there was a book called *Breath Prayers for African Americans* that has a black woman on the cover. Instructions on what to do after reading the book were encouraging.

The instructions were as follows: Choose a suitable prayer to use throughout your day. Repeat it so that you can say it to yourself in one breath, breathe in and out. Each breath is a prayer. In this way you will pray without ceasing, aware of God walking through each experience with you. Unity teaches that our thoughts are prayers and we are praying all the time. It can also mean you praise God even though things are not going your way at the moment. The words will stay the same, but each breath you pray will be unique in the way you mean it to God. And you will maintain a constant connection with Him.

Daily devotion is a must in the life of a Christian woman. The women of the Bible had their way and we twenty-first century women have ours. I thank God daily for the tools to get to know him better. For the individuals that use computers there are tools such as Smart Phone Apps and various websites to assist you with your devotional time.

MM/DD/YY

Dear Friends,

Thank you for agreeing to participate in completing the Women of the Bible

Questionnaire needed for my study group/women's conference.

Please complete the questionnaire and mail it back to me by mm/dd/yy. I have enclosed a self-addressed stamped envelope for your convenience.

I thank you in advance for your prompt attention.

Sincerely,

Your Name

Note: These electronic documents both letter and questionnaire are both available at www.sacpr.com

Appendix A

Women of the Bible

Questionnaire

The purpose of this questionnaire is to help us understand how you and other women feel about daily devotions, so that we can share and use the tools available to improve our relationships with Christ to grow spiritually.

Please answer each question as completely as possible. This questionnaire will be used only as research material for your Bible Study, and your individual answers will be held in strict confidence, no one will be individually identified in our report. So please feel free to tell us anything you think we may need to know that can help others.

Please put a check mark (√) next to your response.

1. Are you _____ Asian American

_____ American Indian

_____ Black/African American

_____ Hispanic

_____ White/Caucasian

_____ Other (please specify)

2. Do you have a personal relationship with Jesus Christ?

_____ Yes

_____ No

_____ Somewhat

_____ Don't know

3.   Do you have daily devotions?

       _____   Yes

       _____   No

       _____   Somewhat

       _____   Don't know

4.   How long have you been having daily devotions?

       _____   1 year or less

       _____   over 1 year, but less than 3 years

       _____   3 to 5 years

       _____   Don't have daily devotions

5. Do you have an understanding of what a daily devotion is?

    _____ Yes

    _____ No

    _____ Somewhat

    _____ Don't know

6. Do you use a study Bible for your daily devotions?

    _____ Yes

    _____ No

    _____ Somewhat

    _____ Don't know

7. Does your Bible offer any (portraits, insight essays or life lessons)?

_____ Yes

_____ No

_____ Somewhat

_____ Don't know

8. Do you read any daily devotional material such as (Daily Bread, Upper Room , Today God is First or Meditating Moments)?

_____ Yes

_____ No

_____ Somewhat

_____ Don't know

9. On a scale of 1 to 10 with 1 representing "mostly unfulfilled" please rate the extent that your expectations have been met by your daily devotions.

(Please circle the most appropriate rating)

    mostly   mostly

unfulfilled 1 2   3   4 5 6 7 8 9 10 fulfilled

10. Would you recommend daily devotion for others?

       _____ Yes

       _____ No

       _____ Somewhat

       _____ Don't know

THANK YOU FOR YOUR HELP

Should you have additional comments, please use the space below to provide them.

_____

_____

_____

_____

_____

_____

Study Notes

CHAPTER 5

SUMMING UP

Thank you! Thank you! Thank you! The opportunity to research and discover how various women of the Bible are the examples for the women of today. My eyes have been opened to personalities and how to deal with the good, the bad and ugly. I was amazed at the intimate side of Jesus and how he encountered women, this makes me feel special. I learned how to understand and share the Scriptures that state how special women really are. The review of this thesis turned book allowed me, as a working woman, to see how the professions are still the same but the duties and responsibilities of women have changed. When conducting my daily devotions I now have a different outlook.

The tools that are available to assist with learning and growing in the word are numerous. There is no reason for any woman to feel deprived because there is so much inexpensive and "free" materials available to help anyone who desires to have a closer relationship with the heavenly father.

A review of Chapter 2 and summing up Jesus' Relationship with Women included some women whose first names were Mary including those in the family, friends and even enemy category. With this portion I wanted to share how Jesus had a relationship with women who didn't have specific names, but he had encounters with them.

When I think of the women of then and now with their professions, I marvel at how we have come full circle. It has been stated prior that the titles may have changed as well as responsibilities of occupations both then and now. When recapping its important to remember that you can work in the home as well on the outside of the home and receive full satisfaction of what your gift, talent, or purpose is. To summarize the working woman if she is an entrepreneur or enterprising women have always had to figure out how to make ends meet.

To help obtain information about women and the word a questionnaire was constructed. This information confirmed that with the right tools women will read and have daily devotions. The summary of results is listed in Appendix B. There was a sample of 20 questionnaires sent out and 14 were returned. The breakdown by percentage of women completing the questionnaire and their comments are listed with a response to each question.

Appendix B

Women of the Bible

Questionnaire

The purpose of this questionnaire is to help us understand how you and other women feel about daily devotions, so that we can share and use the tools available to improve our relationships with Christ to grow spiritually.

Please answer each question as completely as possible. This questionnaire will be used only as research material, and your individual answers will be held in strict confidence and no one will be individually identified in our report. So please feel free to tell us anything you think we may need to know that can help others.

Please put a check mark (√) next to your response.

1.   Are you   _____ Asian American
                      _____ American Indian

___11___ Black/African American 79%

_____ Hispanic

___3___ White/Caucasian 21%
_____ Other (please specify_____)

When I inquired about who did not return their questionnaire, there were three African/American women who confessed and it was interesting to note that two were under the age of thirty and one stated that she just didn't really think about doing it.

2. Do you have a personal relationship with Jesus Christ?
___13___ Yes 93%
_____ No
___7___ Somewhat 7%
_____ Don't know

This question puzzled a few of the participants because the language "personal relationship" does not mean the same for the women of color who are older.

I was told by many of the seniors "I've been knowing God a long time", now, the Christian community knows it means something totally different from what she was saying, so I consider this a cultural and generation barrier for responding to the questions.

3.   Do you have daily devotions?

_____7_____	Yes	50%
_____2_____	No	14%
_____5_____	Somewhat	36%
_____	Don't know	

There were comments made from the participants that their basic prayer at night or grace during meals were sufficient for daily devotions. They did more on Wednesday because of Bible Study.

4.   How long have you been having daily devotions?

_____1_____	1 year or less	7%
_____	over 1 year, but less than 3 years	
_____11____	3 to 5 years	79%
_____2_____	Don't have daily devotions	14%

Written comments were: "I have been knowing the Lord longer than you have been born." This comment was to let me know that it was a senior who did not want me to think she was a new Christian and that she wanted to know, why would I ask a silly question like that. This also told me that the more seasoned Christian has a problem with longevity of being a Christian and what should have been expected of one who is not on milk (baby) versus a solid food Christian (mature).

5.   Do you have an understanding of what a daily devotion is?

___14___	Yes	100%
_____	No	
_____	Somewhat	
_____	Don't know	

The response at 100% really made me wonder if they really knew what I was asking. I wanted to know: Do you have a song, scripture, prayer and daily reading of something in your devotion? I didn't spell it out but they all responded, **yes**. So who am I too judge if they say they do or they don't.

6.   Do you use a study Bible for your daily devotions?

5	Yes	36%
6	No	43%
2	Somewhat	14%
1	Don't know	7%

I had given 12 of the people birthday presents of the *Women of Color Study Bible,* and had requested they use it for devotional time; so it was interesting to see the percentage who responded **no**. When I was sharing my results with one participant she told me that it was too pretty and she didn't want to mark in it or take notes in it. She stated the color of the Bible and how much attention she receives when she uses it in public was why she does not want to use it. No! This is not what I wanted to happen with the *Women of Color Study Bible* it was given to help them identify with the content.

7.   Does your Bible offer any (portraits, insight essays or life lessons)

8	Yes	57%
6	No	43%
	Somewhat	
	Don't know	

Many of the study Bibles today have interesting notes and messages along the margins to encourage the reader or support the message. Because I know 12 of the people had study Bibles, it was encouraging to know that maybe 11 of them were using them properly.

8.   Do you read any daily devotional material such as (*Daily Bread, Upper Room, Today, God is First or Meditating Moments*)?

_____11_____	Yes*	79%
_____2_____	No	14%
_____1_____	Somewhat	7%
_____	Don't know	

*This response was encouraging since much material is *free* at churches, doctors offices, hospitals and any place that has reading materials. For the computer savvy or literate individuals there are many daily electronic versions such as *Today God is First* (TGIF) and *Meditating Moments* are on your screen each morning to help you get your work day started off right.

9. On a scale of 1 to 10 with 1 representing "mostly unfulfilled" please rate the extent that your expectations have been met by your daily devotions.

(Please circle the most appropriate rating)

<pre>
      mostly   mostly
   unfulfilled 1 2   3   4 5 6   7 8 9 10 fulfilled
                      1   1 1   3 4   4
</pre>

The response to their *daily walk* is what I was alluding to with this question. I know that we all need to continue to grow in the word and we can never have enough. So their responses let me know that many would say *I'm just getting by* at ratings 3-5 with meeting expectations and 8-10 feel as if they are at the top of the game relative to devotion. What many women fail to remember is that there is always growth in the word.

10. Would you recommend daily devotion for others?

___13___	Yes	93%
___1___	No	7%
_____	Somewhat	
_____	Don't know	

The responses from this question were simple. I was merely asking if they would be a witness without really coming out and asking it. I asked because if a woman shares a message from her daily devotion, then she is being a witness. There was one person who did respond **no** and that may be attributed to age. They may have been an older person or a younger person who just did not understand the question (see comments).

THANK YOU FOR YOUR HELP

Should you have additional comments, please use the space below to provide them.

- Daily thanks to our Lord; Meditate, Study.
- My daily devotion needs to improve, but I focus on Christ daily. Through the power of the Holy Spirit, I have a longing to learn more about Jesus and to be more like Him. I'm able to witness for him. Through the power of the Holy Spirit I'm growing strong in the Lord.
- What I want to do is to have a better relationship with the Lord. This survey woke me up about having devotions on a regular basis.

- Reading the daily word, and the women daily devotional helps me get my day started after my morning prayer.
- I don't personally do daily readings but, when I did it was just from a Sunday School lesson or reading Joyce Meyers or something like that. I know in my heart I need to get back to this I just find every reason not too. I know that is the devil. God Bless! Thanks for making me realize the devil has a lot of hold on me.
- Always acknowledge God with your words and deeds. God Bless!

Comments: Many did not write comments on the back because they didn't follow through with reading the form completely, I found that to be true on several of the African/American questionnaires. When I confronted many of them about the comments on the questionnaire they informed me that they didn't know there was anything on the back and they just checked the spaces and mailed it in. As a researcher/author I definitely see a flaw in the questionnaire by not putting on the bottom of the page, *please turn over*.

The primary objective of the questionnaire was to show how women use devotional tools as support for their daily devotionals. Something as simple as picking up two Daily Bread or Upper Room books, to keep one for yourself and to give one to a friend, starts the sharing and then comes the witnessing and giving of praise reports. Women have to encourage each other and support them not just with your time and for many just a listening ear. From this research I am realizing from their responses that CDs or tapes are great for the seniors who have a hard time reading and I can donate headphones to the ones who are hard of hearing to listen to messages. This gives them the message for the week from the pastor so they have something to mediate on during the week. I am going to expand this outreach ministry to the sick and shut in as well.

Women will grow using the tools provided to support their growth in the word, by just knowing *which* tool to use and not use something that is too advanced for a baby trying to be an adult in the word.

Well, I am at the end of summing up. But I stopped and screamed and shouted because I was handwriting all of this down and then I had a plan to key it into the computer. As I was keying and having to reread the information I wrote down it was a great feeling.

But as I reminisce about the last few weeks of reading the memories of researching and trying to find the right material really made it difficult to leave it as it was because I have grown so much and I don't talk like I used too and now I know my purpose. The real hands on of getting information together about this paper turned book were the people in the last days and incidents where I interacted and what I responded to. Each of these activities reflected right back to several of the stories.

Listed are a few of those incidents and if you notice I refer to them as incidents not accidents because God doesn't make things happen by accident. He has a purpose for everything that he does. There were promises made to a young person on visiting a college and the pressure of completing my book was upon me which would make me lose two days of editing time. However, I did it and it made a lifetime memory for a young person (Herodias).

The availability to console an elderly neighbor on losing a sibling, spending time with her by talking and reassuring her that God loves her and that she needed to keep the faith. This was two days away from book deadline as I helped plan funeral arrangements and ensured that she was taken care of with transportation and hotel arrangements to travel out of town to the funeral.

I encouraged her over and over again that God had not deserted her that she has a son and brothers who need her. (Sorrowing woman) While doing work on my house a godly worker confides in me about losing his wife and how lonely he has become. I was available to listen and share with him about women he may come across. (Gomer).

Personally during these last few weeks I started feeling sick, exhausted and was diagnosed with a medical condition that will require additional medication for 90 days to see if it can get under control.

I related instantly to the (suffering woman). Also, during this time I am having work done on my house and I asked the Lord to put his hand on my house to keep the culprits out as I took bids for the work and he sent a Christian woman the only woman business owner in her profession who gave me a bid that was half or less than what the others quoted and every person she has subcontracted to do work has been a Christian as well. (Virtuous woman)

Within a week of trying to complete this book *I lived it*. It got to the point that I had to stand up and shout, "Lord, order my steps!" I don't know what the Lord has in store for me, but I know it will be a blessing. I let go and let God write this paper turned book.

I hope that many will accept that God gave me what he wanted me to share for others to know. It has been both exciting and enjoyable to do something that will help others grow spiritually. I have taken this information and restructured it by adding pictures to capture the lives of women who reflect the good, the bad and the ugly then and now. Please look for this release to take your devotion to another level. This information is to be used as "real" not "fictional" reading material. Amen!

Notes

Chapter 1
1. Mize, Mary E. Profiles of Biblical Women. (Cadiz: Barkely, 1984.) 57.
2. MacArthur, John. Twelve Extraordinary Women. (Nashville: Nelson, 2005.) 69.
3. Ruth 1:16
4. Mize 65.
5. McArthur 88.
6. Mize 67.
7. Richards, L[arry] S[ue]. Every Woman In The Bible. (Nashville: Nelson, 2005) 109.
8. Richards 150.
9. Ieron, Julie A. Names of Women of the Bible. (Chicago: Moody, 1982) 33.
10. Mize 106.
11. Richards 251.
12. Lawson, Marjorie. Women of Color Study Bible. (Iowa Falls: World, 1999) 22.
13. Genesis 29:19
14. Mize 31.
15. Romans 3:23
16. Genesis 3:3
17. Lawson 22.
18. Lawson 807.
19. Mize 11.
20. Richards 13.
21. Higgs, Liz C. Bad Girls of the Bible. (Colorado Springs: Waterbrook, 2000) 37.
22. Higgs 50.
23. Richards 103.
24. Gruen, Dietrich. Who's Who in the Bible. (Lincolnwood: Publications, 1995) 71.
25. I Kings 21:23
26. 2 Samuel 11:26-27
27. Lawson 250.
28. Judges 4:9
29. Higgs 52.
30. Essex, Barbara J. Bad Girls of the Bible. Cleveland: Pilgrim, 1999.
31. Essex 22.
32. Genesis 27: 43-75
33. Essex 27.
34. Mark 1:4
35. Mark 6:22-23
36. Ieron 192.
37. Gruen 291.

38. Joshua 2:2-3
39. Richards 166.
40. Genesis 38:26.
41. Richards 57.
42. Genesis 19:12
43. Higgs 72.
44. Job 2:7
45. Richards 151.
46. Essex 74.
47. Job 2:9-10

Chapter 2
1. Luke 1:28
2. Luke 2:49
3. Ashker, Helene. Jesus Cares for Women. (Colorado Springs: NAV Press, 1987)
   46.
4. Luke 7:14
5. Ashker 49-50.
6. Lawson 714.
7. Higgs 243.
8. Lawson 735.
9. Essex 93.
10. John 8:4-5.
11. Lawson 764.
12. John 8:7
13. John 8: 9-11.
14. Essex 95.
15. Matthew 18:7
16. Lawson 696.
17. Richards 191.

Chapter 3
1. Richards 166.
2. Luke 21:3
3. Luke 10:42
4. McArthur 146.
5. John 4:11-12.
6. John 4:14
7. Lawson 759.
8. John 4:17
9. Higgs 95.
10. John 4:18
11. John 4:25-26.
12. MacArthur 49.
13. MacArthur 151.
14. Higgs 99.
15. Matthew 26:7

16. Higgs 223.
17. Matthew 26:9
18. Luke 7:44-46.
19. Lawson 705.
20. Higgs 233.
21. Deut. 15:4-5.
22. Essex 99.
23. Higgs 137.
24. Acts 5:3
25. Lawson 781.
26. Acts 5:7:9
27. Acts 5:10
28. Essex 101.

Chapter 4
1. MacArthur 27.
2. Mize 17.
3. Gruen 267.
4. 2 John 7, 9-11
5. James 4:7
6. Ephesians 6:13
7. Psalm 18:28-30
8. Psalm 18:17
9. Marshall, Catherine. God's Promises for Women. (Nashville: Countryman, 199) 145..
10. Omartian,Stormie. The Prayer That Changes Everything. (Eugene: Harvest, 2004) 288.
11. Omartian 290.
12. Omartian 293.
13. Breathnach, Sarah B. Simple Abundance A Daybook of Comfort and Joy. (New York: Warner 1995) 2.
14. Harrison, Shawn. Touch Points for Women. (Wheaton: Tyndale, 1998) 326.
15. Dick, D[an] N[ancy]. God's Word for Simple Abundance. (Urhichsville: Barbour, 2000) 6.
16. Bryant, Stephen D. The Upper Room Daily Devotional Guide. (Nashville: Canada Post, 2005) 40.
17. Lawson 5.
18. Otis, Rose. The Listening Heart. (Hagerstown: Review, 1993) 427.
19. Houghton, Frank. Quiet Time an Inter-varsity Guidebook for Daily Devotions. (Madison: Inter-Varsity, 1975) 1.
20. Jordan, Edna G. Breath Prayers for African Americans. (Colorado Springs: Honor Books, 2004) 7.

Resources

Ashker, Helene. Jesus Cares for Women. Colorado Springs: NAV Pres, 1987.

Breathnach, Sarah B. Simple Abundance A Daybook of Comfort and Joy. New York: Warner, 1995.

Bryant, Stephen D. The Upper Room Daily Devotional Guide. Nashville: Canada Post, 2005.

Christenson, Evelyn. What Happens When Women Pray. Wheaton: Tyndale, 1971..

Dick, D[an] N[ancy]. God's Word for Simple Abundance. uhrichsville: Barbour, 2000.

Essex, Barbara J. Bad Girls of the Bible. Cleveland: Pilgrim, 1999.

Felder, Cain H. The Original African Heritage Study Bible. Nashville: Winston,1993.

Gruen, Dietrich. Who's Who in the Bible. Lincolnwood: Publications, 1995.

Harrison, Shawn. Touch Points for Women. Wheaton: Tyndale, 1998.

Higgs, Liz C Bad Girls of the bible. Colorado Springs: Waterbrook, 1999. ---,ed. Really Bad Grls of the Bible. Colorado Springs: Waterbrook, 2000.

Houghton, Frank. Quiet Time An Intervarsity Guidebook for Daily Devotions. Madison: Intervarsity, 1975.

Ieron, Julie A. Names of Women of The Bible. chicago: Moody, 1982.

Jordan, Edna G. Breath Prayers for African Americans. Colorado Springs: Honor Books, 2004.

Lawson, Marjorie. Women of Color Study Bible. Iowa Falls: World, 1999.

Lockyer, Herbert. Nelson's Illustrated Bible Dictionary. Nashville: Nelson, 1986.

Lucao, Max. The Inspirational Study Bible. Minneapolis: Word, 1995.

MacArthur, John. Twelve Extraordinary Women. Nashville: Nelson 2005.

Marshall, Catherine. God's Promises for Women: Nashville: Countryman, 1999.

Mize, Mary E. Profiles of Biblical Women. Cadiz: Barkley, 1984.

Omartian, Stormie. The Prayer that Changes Everything. Eugene: Harvest, 2004.

Otis, Rose. The Listening Heart. Hagerstown: Review 1993.

Price, Eugenia. God Speaks to Women Now. Grand Rapids: Zondervan, 1964.

Richards, L[arry] S[ue]. Every Woman in The Bible. Nashville: Nelson, 1999.

Women of the Bible

the good, the bad, & ugly...

then and now

BY DR. SHARON CANNON

Contact Dr. Sharon Cannon: www.sacpr.com

Made in the USA
Columbia, SC
06 July 2019